Procurement and Contract Strategies

This document provides guidance for users of NEC in determining the procurement and contract strategies to achieve planned outcomes and in the application of contracts from the NEC3 family in meeting these strategies

An NEC document

April 2013

Construction Clients' Board endorsement of NEC3

The Construction Clients' Board recommends that public sector organisations use the NEC3 contracts when procuring construction. Standardising use of this comprehensive suite of contracts should help to deliver efficiencies across the public sector and promote behaviours in line with the principles of *Achieving Excellence in Construction*.

Cabinet Office UK

NEC is a division of Thomas Telford Ltd, which is a wholly owned subsidiary of the Institution of Civil Engineers (ICE), the owner and developer of the NEC.

The NEC is a family of standard contracts, each of which has these characteristics:

- Its use stimulates good management of the relationship between the two parties to the contract and, hence, of the work included in the contract.
- It can be used in a wide variety of commercial situations, for a wide variety of types of work and in any location.
- It is a clear and simple document – using language and a structure which are straightforward and easily understood.

ISBN (complete box set) 978 0 7277 5867 5
ISBN (this document) 978 0 7277 5941 2

First edition June 2005
Reprinted 2007, 2008
Revised edition December 2009
Reprinted 2010
Reprinted with amendments 2013

British Library Cataloguing in Publication Data for this publication is available from the British Library.

Typeset by Academic + Technical, Bristol

Printed and bound in Great Britain by Bell & Bain Limited, Glasgow, UK

CONTENTS

FOREWORD

I was delighted to be asked to write the Foreword for the NEC3 Contracts.

I have followed the outstanding rise and success of NEC contracts for a number of years now, in particular during my tenure as the 146th President of the Institution of Civil Engineers, 2010/11.

In my position as UK Government's Chief Construction Adviser, I am working with Government and industry to ensure Britain's construction sector is equipped with the knowledge, skills and best practice it needs in its transition to a low carbon economy. I am promoting innovation in the sector, including in particular the use of Building Information Modelling (BIM) in public sector construction procurement; and the synergy and fit with the collaborative nature of NEC contracts is obvious. The Government's construction strategy is a very significant investment and NEC contracts will play an important role in setting high standards of contract preparation, management and the desirable behaviour of our industry.

In the UK, we are faced with having to deliver a 15–20 per cent reduction in the cost to the public sector of construction during the lifetime of this Parliament. Shifting mind-set, attitude and behaviour into best practice NEC processes will go a considerable way to achieving this.

Of course, NEC contracts are used successfully around the world in both public and private sector projects; this trend seems set to continue at an increasing pace. NEC contracts are, according to my good friend and NEC's creator Dr Martin Barnes CBE, about better management of projects. This is quite achievable and I encourage you to understand NEC contracts to the best you can and exploit the potential this offers us all.

Peter Hansford

UK Government's Chief Construction Adviser
Cabinet Office

PREFACE

The NEC contracts are the only suite of standard contracts designed to facilitate and encourage good management of the projects on which they are used. The experience of using NEC contracts around the world is that they really make a difference. Previously, standard contracts were written mainly as legal documents best left in the desk drawer until costly and delaying problems had occurred and there were lengthy arguments about who was to blame.

The language of NEC contracts is clear and simple, and the procedures set out are all designed to stimulate good management. Foresighted collaboration between all the contributors to the project is the aim. The contracts set out how the interfaces between all the organisations involved will be managed – from the client through the designers and main contractors to all the many subcontractors and suppliers.

Versions of the NEC contract are specific to the work of professional service providers such as project managers and designers, to main contractors, to subcontractors and to suppliers. The wide range of situations covered by the contracts means that they do not need to be altered to suit any particular situation.

The NEC contracts are the first to deal specifically and effectively with management of the inevitable risks and uncertainties which are encountered to some extent on all projects. Management of the expected is easy, effective management of the unexpected draws fully on the collaborative approach inherent in the NEC contracts.

Most people working on projects using the NEC contracts for the first time are hugely impressed by the difference between the confrontational characteristics of traditional contracts and the teamwork engendered by the NEC. The NEC does not include specific provisions for dispute avoidance. They are not necessary. Collaborative management itself is designed to avoid disputes and it really works.

It is common for the final account for the work on a project to be settled at the time when the work is finished. The traditional long period of expensive professional work after completion to settle final payments just is not needed.

The NEC contracts are truly a massive change for the better for the industries in which they are used.

Dr Martin Barnes CBE

Originator of the NEC contracts

ACKNOWLEDGEMENTS

The third edition of the NEC Procurement and Contract Strategies was drafted by Robert Gerrard working on behalf of the Institution of Civil Engineers, with the assistance of members of the NEC Panel.

The original NEC was designed and drafted by Dr Martin Barnes then of Coopers and Lybrand with the assistance of Professor J. G. Perry then of the University of Birmingham, T. W. Weddell then of Travers Morgan Management, T. H. Nicholson, Consultant to the Institution of Civil Engineers, A. Norman then of the University of Manchester Institute of Science and Technology and P. A. Baird, then Corporate Contracts Consultant, Eskom, South Africa.

The members of the NEC Panel are:

> N. C. Shaw, FCIPS, CEng, MIMechE (Chairman)
> F. Alderson, BA (Melb), Solicitor
> P. A. Baird, BSc, CEng, FICE, M(SA)ICE, MAPM
> M. Codling, BSc, ICIOB, MAPM
> L. T. Eames, BSc, FRICS, FCIOB
> M. Garratt, BSc(Hons), MRICS, FCIArb
> J. J. Lofty, MRICS

NEC Consultant:

> R. A. Gerrard BSc(Hons), FRICS, FCIArb, FCInstCES

Secretariat

> J. M. Hawkins, BA(Hons), MSc
> S. Hernandez, BSc, MSc

AMENDMENTS APRIL 2013

The following amendments have been made to the December 2009 edition. Full details of all amendments are available on www.neccontract.com.

Page	Line
1	14 insert: 'a Professional Services Short Contract'
2, 3	Table 1 insert new 1st column 2nd column amend all dates to '(April 2013)' Insert new sentence at end of description for PSC Insert new row for PSSC after PSC entry Insert new sentence at end of description for TSC last column add in TSC after 1st sentence 'This service is often provided to a client's existing asset such as a building or some infrastructure, and also perhaps services within an existing asset such as planned/unplanned maintenance, or catering'
5	Para 8, Line 6 insert: ', PSSC' after 'are the PSC'
21	Para 5, Line 1 insert: ', PSSC' after 'ECC, ECSC, PSC' Para 5, Line 2 delete: 'even' before 'SSC'
	Figures 1–15 minor amends

Outline of NEC

NEC is a modern day family of contracts that facilitates the implementation of sound project management principles and practices as well as defining legal relationships. Key to the successful use of NEC is users adopting the desired cultural transition. The main aspect of this transition is moving away from a reactive and hindsight-based decision-making and management approach to one that is foresight based, encouraging a creative environment with pro-active and collaborative relationships.

NEC has matured from being a revolutionary contract in the early 1990s with some interest and use from forward thinking organisations seeking change in how they go about engaging suppliers in a non-adversarial manner. NEC2 was published in 1995 and was increasingly the contract of choice of many organisations in the United Kingdom. NEC3 is the result of feedback from industry on many years of successful use and is the first time that the complete integrated set of NEC documents have been launched at the same time. The family has been expanded to provide a Term Service Contract, a Term Service Short Contract, a Professional Services Short Contract, a Supply Contract, a Supply Short Contract and Framework Contract, all complemented with the standard NEC approach of including guidance notes and flow charts.

NEC is a family of standard contracts, each of which has these characteristics:

- Its use stimulates good management of the relationship between the two parties to the contract and, hence, of the work included in the contract.

- It can be used in a wide variety of commercial situations, for a wide variety of types of work and in any location.

- It is a clear and simple document – using language and a structure which are straightforward and easily understood.

NEC is an integrated set of contract documents that are designed to provide Clients and their suppliers with processes focussed on achieving desired, planned outcomes. The intention is that use of NEC will lead more frequently to achievement of Clients' objectives in terms of its ultimate quality, performance, cost and time aspects. It should also be possible to set more rigorous targets for these objectives with greater confidence in achieving them.

NEC is drafted on a relational contracting basis that embodies efficient management processes. It is the belief that collaborative working across the entire supply chain optimises the likely outcomes when compared with a typically fragmented and non-integrated approach. NEC gives the tools to the users to draw out their skills to apply to the environment they are working in.

NEC is intended for global application and is effectively drafted on a neutral jurisdiction basis to achieve this goal. Some United Kingdom amendments are included in secondary Options to meet particular governing legislation and a similar process can be followed where necessary to suit other jurisdictions.

This guide is aimed at both new and experienced users of NEC and the purpose is to assist in the application of NEC when selecting procurement and contract strategies to achieve project objectives.

NEC3 contracts

The current list of published NEC3 contracts and a brief description of each is stated in Table 1 below.

	NEC Title	Abbreviation	Brief Description
Works	NEC3 Engineering and Construction Contract April 2013	ECC	This contract should be used for the appointment of a contractor for engineering and construction work, including any level of design responsibility.
	NEC3 Engineering and Construction Subcontract April 2013	ECS	This contract should be used for the appointment of a subcontractor for engineering and construction work where the contractor has been appointed under the ECC.
	NEC3 Engineering and Construction Short Contract April 2013	ECSC	This contract is an alternative to ECC and is for use with contracts which do not require sophisticated management techniques, comprise straightforward work and impose only low risks on both client and a contractor.
	NEC3 Engineering and Construction Short Subcontract April 2013	ECSS	This contract can be used as a subcontract to ECC or ECSC. It should be used with contracts that do not require sophisticated management techniques, comprise straightforward work and impose only low risks on both the contractor and subcontractor.
Services	NEC3 Professional Services Contract April 2013	PSC	This contract should be used for the appointment of a supplier to provide professional services. Its use is not limited to projects where other NEC contracts are being used. It can be used stand alone or as a subcontract to another NEC contract.
	NEC3 Professional Services Short Contract April 2013	PSSC	This contract should be used for the appointment of a supplier to provide professional services. It is an alternative to the PSC and is for use with contracts which do not require sophisticated management techniques, comprise straightforward work and impose only low risks on both the client and consultant.
	NEC3 Term Service Contract April 2013	TSC	This contract should be used for the appointment of a supplier for a period of time to manage and provide a service. This service is often provided to a client's existing asset such as a building or some infrastructure, and also perhaps services within an existing asset such as planned/unplanned maintenance, or catering. It is designed for use in a wide variety of situations such as Facilities Management (FM) and highways maintenance.

Part 1
What is NEC?

Part 2
NEC3 Procurement and
Contract Strategies

Part 3
Other Procurement
Aspects

	NEC Title	Abbreviation	Brief Description
Services	NEC3 Term Service Short Contract April 2013	TSSC	This contract should be used for the appointment of a supplier for a period of time to manage and provide a service. It is an alternative to the TSC and is for use with contracts which do not require sophisticated management techniques, comprise straightforward work and impose only low risks on both client and a contractor.
Supply	NEC3 Supply Contract April 2013	SC	This contract should be used for local and international procurement of high-value goods and related services including design.
Supply	NEC3 Supply Short Contract April 2013	SSC	This contract should be used for local and international procurement of goods under a single order or on a batch order basis and is for use with contracts which do not require sophisticated management techniques and impose only low risks on both client and a supplier.
	NEC3 Framework Contract April 2013	FC	This contract should be used for the appointment of one or more suppliers to carry out construction work or to provide design or advisory services on an 'as instructed' basis over a set term.
	NEC3 Adjudicator's Contract April 2013	AC	This contract should be used for the appointment of an Adjudicator to decide disputes under the NEC family of contracts. It may also be used for the appointment of an Adjudicator under other forms of contract.

Table 1. NEC3 contracts.

With the exception of the AC, all other NEC contracts are drafted for use in a multi-party partnering arrangement utilising the provisions of Option X12 Partnering.

The flexibility of NEC in the various procurement and contract strategies available is described in Part 2.

Option structure

The ECC, ECS, PSC and TSC offer up a range of Options to select from that builds up the contract terms to suit the works or services. At the heart of the contract conditions are the core clauses, which contain the essential common terms. To this must be added a main Option, which will determine the particular payment mechanism. Finally, the selected secondary Options are combined with the core and main Option clauses to provide a complete contract.

This approach gives even greater choice to contracting parties to assemble the appropriate contract conditions to suit. The ECC, ECS, PSC and TSC offer different basic allocations of financial risk between the parties through the main Options.

The ECC main Options and a brief description of each is as follows.

- Options A and B: these are priced contracts with the risk of carrying out the work at the agreed prices being largely borne by the Contractor.

- Options C and D: these are target cost contracts in which the out-turn financial risks are shared between the Client and the Contractor in an agreed proportion.

- Options E and F: these are cost reimbursable types of contract with the financial risk being largely taken the Client.

The comparative availability of the main Options in ECC, ECS, PSC and TSC is shown in Table 2.

Option Title	ECC	ECS	PSC	TSC
A. Priced contract with activity schedule	✓	✓	✓	✓ with Price List
B. Priced contract with bill of quantities	✓	✓	×	×
C. Target contract with activity schedule	✓	✓	✓	✓ with Price List
D. Target contract with bill of quantities	✓	✓	×	×
E. Cost reimbursable contract	✓	✓	✓ time based	✓
F. Management contract	✓	×	×	×
G. Term contract	×	×	✓	×

Table 2. Availability of main Options in NEC3 contracts.

Part 2   NEC3 Procurement and Contract Strategies

Sustainable procurement of works, services and supply relies upon making value for money decisions over the life of the asset and not solely on capital costs. A value for money solution to meet user requirements relies upon the optimum combination of whole-life costs and quality.

Any procurement strategy should identify the best way of achieving the project objectives, taking into account the likes of key objectives, constraints, funding, risk and asset ownership. It is the optimum balance of these factors that one strives for.

The procurement route is the means of achieving the procurement strategy. This will include the contract strategy that best meets the client's needs.

The contract strategy will determine the level of integration of design, construction and maintenance for a project. This should support the main project objectives in terms of the likes of risk allocation, incentivisation and delivery.

There are many procurement routes available including traditional, design and build, prime contracting, management contracts and private finance initiative/public–private partnership (PFI/PPP). The NEC is designed to be flexible enough to work in most currently available procurement routes.

Traditional approaches

The traditional approach with many projects, particularly in the construction industry, is to have design as a separate function from construction.

This is less common for the supply of goods or plant where it is usually the supplier who carries our product design.

Figure 1 shows a simple relationship between a Client and a Consultant or Contractor for pre-construction or construction related services. The Client could be one of public or private standing and the Consultant or Contractor can in turn subcontract services to suit. The contract could be for the likes of design, project management, cost consultancy, environmental, audit, facilitation, management consultancy or architectural services. The NEC contracts that could be used are the PSC, PSSC, TSC or TSSC and this approach can be used on a one-off project or a series of projects.

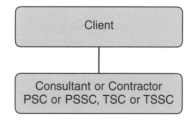

Figure 1. Single appointment for pre-construction or construction-related services.

Part 1
What is NEC?

Part 2
NEC3 Procurement and
Contract Strategies

Part 3
Other Procurement
Aspects

Figure 2 shows a simple relationship between a Client and a Supplier for the local and international procurement of goods. The Client could be one of public or private standing and could also be a Consultant or Contractor. The Supplier can in turn subcontract the supply of goods to suit. The NEC contracts that could be used are the SC or SSC and this approach can be used on a one-off project or a series of projects.

The SC could be for the likes of purchasing transformers, turbine rotors, rolling stock, loading bridges, marine vessels, transmission plant and cable mining machinery; the SSC could be for the likes of purchasing stationery, printer supplies, laboratory chemicals, tools, desks, chairs, portable test equipment, raw materials, pre-manufactured materials or plant.

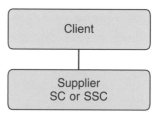

Figure 2. Single appointment for supply of goods.

Figure 3 shows another simple contractual relationship this time for construction works to be carried out for a Client by a Contractor. Again, the Client could be one of public or private standing and the Contractor can in turn subcontract works to suit. The contract could be for constructing any construction or engineering works. The NEC contracts that should be used are the ECC, ECSC, TSC or TSSC and this approach can be used on a one-off project or a series of projects.

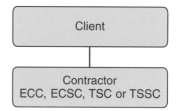

Figure 3. Single appointment for construction works.

The classic traditional contract in the construction industry is a consultant designing works on behalf of a Client who engages a Contractor to construct them, as shown in Figure 4. Under ECC, ECSC, TSC or TSSC, the Contractor is responsible for the quality of his workmanship, however under ECC, the Client has the safeguard of engaging a Supervisor whose role is to check that the materials and workmanship meet the contracted quality levels.

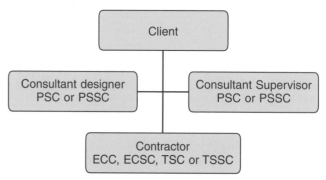

Figure 4. Multiple appointment of suppliers.

More realistically, there will be many organisations involved in even a simple construction project and Figure 5 below demonstrates the cascading NEC contracts in such a relationship.

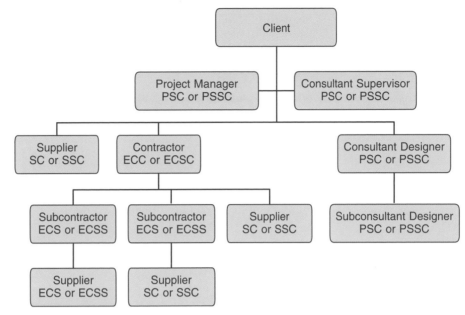

Figure 5. Cascading NEC contracts for works project.

Design and build

There are a number of variants of design and build contracting, including just design and build (D&B), design, build and operate (DBO) and design, build, operate and maintain (DBOM).

In D&B a single Contractor acts as the sole point of responsibility to a Client for the design, management and delivery of a project, on time, within budget and usually in accordance with a performance specification. Figure 6 shows a typical D&B project organisation for a single project. If a Client requires Contractor self-certification of the quality of the works, then the Supervisor instead becomes a function of the Contractor.

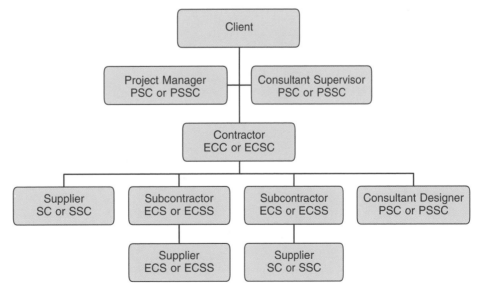

Figure 6. Typical D&B project organisation.

In DBO the Contractor operates the asset over a compliance period primarily to prove the contracted assumptions. The contract strategy for this can be one of two approaches, with the choice largely being down to length of the operating period. If a relatively short operating period is required then the D&B element of the project could be encompassed as a section of the whole of the works within the ECC with the operating period of, say, one year being a second section. Payments for the design, construction and operation would follow the chosen ECC payment option.

If the operating period was a considerable length of time then it may be preferable to enter into two contracts, ideally at the same time, one to D&B under ECC and the other to operate under TSC. Figure 6 is still representative of the D&B element of the works with Figure 7 indicating the TSC contractual relationships. The assumption here is that no further design is required in this period, though of course this could be provided on a subcontracting basis if required.

DBOM is where the asset is also operated and maintained by the Contractor for (usually) an extended period of time of 5, 10, 15 years or more. In this scenario, it is more likely that the two contract approach, with TSC in place to maintain the asset in a certain state, would be the preferred route.

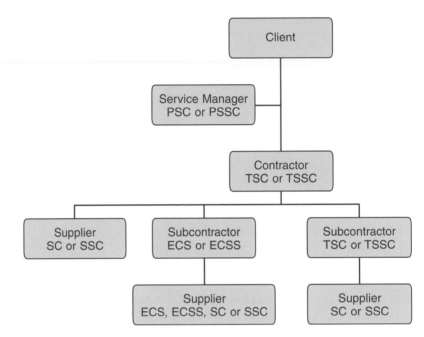

Figure 7. Typical D&B project organisation for operating period.

Prime contracting

Prime contracting is conceptually very similar to D&B and is where a single Contractor again acts as the sole point of responsibility to a Client for the management and delivery of a construction project, on time, within budget (this time defined over the lifetime of a project) and in accordance with (usually) a performance specification. Often Clients will use this model where they require the Contractor to demonstrate, during the initial operating period, that the operating cost and performance parameters can be met in accordance with a pre-agreed cost model.

The contractual relationships for prime contracting are as those for D&B, DBO or DBOM, as applicable. A distinguishing feature of prime contracting in the United Kingdom from D&B is that often the design requirements are to deliver the performance requirement for which the asset was intended, whereas the level of reasonable skill and care is often the chosen norm under the D&B variants. The level of design responsibility can be chosen easily whichever NEC contract is used, however, the risk profile of these are in reality quite different.

Management contracts

Management type contracts include management contracting and construction management; both are catered for in NEC. In reality a management contract structure is similar to a traditional contract, where the main Contractor subcontracts works out. He can carry out as much design and/or construction of the works as he desires, but this should be listed in Contract Data part two as a lump sum total. This stated total, together with the package Contractor's costs, are added together and the management Contractor's Fee is applied to this amount. This total is the Price that the Client pays. Figure 8 illustrates this management contracting relationship.

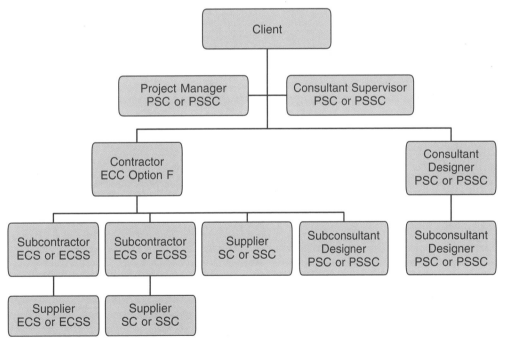

Figure 8. Typical management contracting relationship.

Construction management can be organised under NEC as demonstrated in Figure 9. Here, the Construction Manager joins the professional team alongside the Project Manager, Supervisor and a Designer. Direct contracts are entered into between the Client and specialist trade contractors, who in turn may subcontract works.

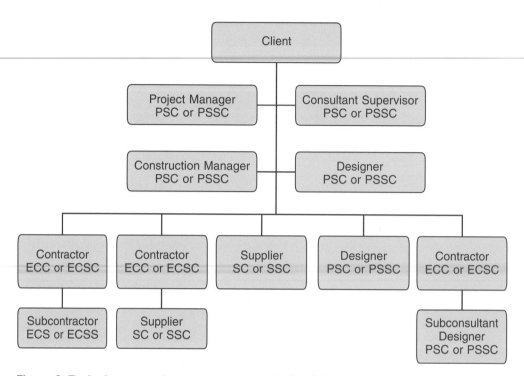

Figure 9. Typical construction management relationship.

PFI/PPP

This procurement route is typically where the public sector Client buys services with defined outputs from the private sector on a long-term basis, typically for 25 years. This will involve maintaining or constructing and maintaining the asset, and the supplier is incentivised in this model to have the highest regard to whole-life costing as they have the risk of operation and maintenance for a substantial period of time.

NEC can be used for all works and services within the supply chain but not for the head contract itself. Traditionally the head contract is a bespoke agreement designed to reflect the specific project. Figure 10 shows how the NEC could be used to design and construct the asset.

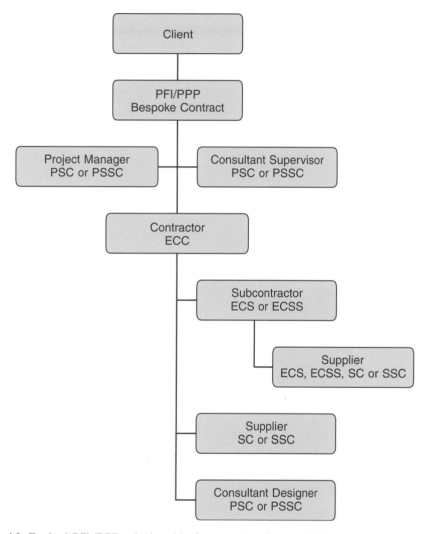

Figure 10. Typical PFI/PPP relationship for construction activities.

Figure 11 shows how the NEC could be used to contractually organise the operation and maintenance (O&M) of the asset.

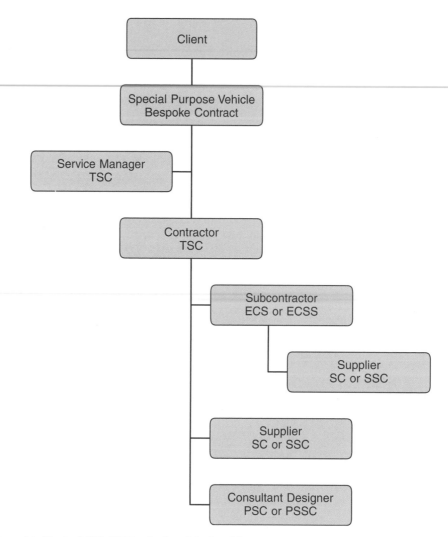

Figure 11. Typical PFI/PPP relationship for O&M activities.

Summary

The extent of types of works, services and supply, and the contractual relations to deliver them, are diverse, but NEC has sufficient flexibility to provide Clients and their suppliers with successful outcomes. Although the use of the entire NEC family is in no way a mandatory requirement, having suppliers engaged on similar and consistent terms, which promote partnering, team working, the principles of lean thinking, a focus on time, cost and quality with a process for dispute avoidance and efficient dispute resolution should disputes arise, will increase the likelihood of mutually satisfactory outcomes for all concerned. NEC terms are a radical departure from traditional drafting approaches and are drafted on a relational contracting basis that embodies efficient management processes.

Part 3   Other Procurement Aspects

Partnering

Recently, Clients have moved away from the traditional route towards partnering, thereby enabling full integration of the design, construction and operation functions.

A partnering contract between two parties only is achieved by using a standard NEC contract. This is a bi-party contract and this NEC contract will be for a contribution of any type, as Contractor or Consultant for example, the work content or objective of which is sufficiently defined to permit a conventional NEC lump sum, bill of quantities or target cost contract to be agreed. Where the content is not so well defined, a cost reimbursable or time-based contract may be used in the early stages.

On some projects or programmes, Clients prefer a multi-party partnering arrangement. Suppliers can be collectively incentivised to achieve project objectives by use of NEC Option X12 Partnering. X12 is used as a secondary Option common to the contracts which each party has with the body which is paying for its work. It is the parties who have this Option included in their contracts that make up the project partnering team. An important distinction between the Partnering Option and other forms of partnering contract is that the Option does not create a multi-party contract, only an arrangement. The structure of the NEC contracts means that X12 only works when an NEC contract is used.

By linking X12 to appropriate bi-party contracts, as shown in Figure 12, it is intended that the NEC can be used

- for partnering for any number of projects (i.e. single project or multi-project),
- locally and internationally,
- for projects of any technical composition and
- as far down the supply chain as required.

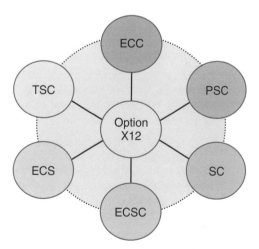

Figure 12. Possible Option X12 Partnering relationship.

Part 1
What is NEC?

Part 2
NEC3 Procurement and Contract Strategies

Part 3
Other Procurement Aspects

Figure 13 shows by use of a star to signify X12, within a single project arrangement for TSC work. Key Partners in any NEC contractual relationship can be drawn out to create the multi-party partnering arrangement. This can of course be extended in a multi-project arrangement.

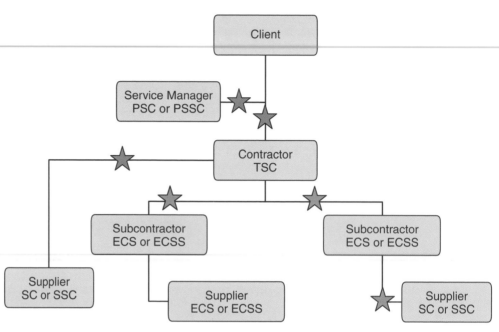

Figure 13. Example of use of Option X12 Partnering.

The common link is X12, which can be used in any combination of NEC contracts, as shown. A Core Group is selected from the Partners. The Partners arise at the point when each Partner's own contract, including the Partnering Option, comes into existence. Not every Partner is necessarily a member of the Core Group. The role of the Core Group is to partner the project to achieve the Client's objectives.

One needs to have regard to the optimum number of Core Group members. Too many members will slow down decision-making. It may be, therefore, that certain groups are represented by one member. For example, there may be five designers on a partnered project but they elect one member to represent them in the Core Group meetings. Clearly, communication between the Partners will be vital.

The model allows essentially the Core Group to work together to achieve the Client's objectives, which are captured in X12. It is the integration of all those suppliers who are able to contribute value to a project that gives the best chance of a successful outcome.

X12 allows for collective or individual incentivisation through the provision of Key Performance Indicators (KPI). A Partner is paid the amount stated if the performance target stated is achieved or improved upon. This is made as part of the amount due in the Partner's own contract. It is not the intention to use negative KPIs in this approach. If collective incentivisation is chosen, if one Partner lets the others down for a particular target by poor performance, then all lose their bonus for that target.

There can be more than one KPI for each Partner. KPIs may apply to one Partner, to several Partners or to all Partners. There is no single answer to what KPIs should or should not be used; NEC through X12 creates a framework for Clients and their Partners to be as creative as they can in incentivising the delivery of the Client's objectives.

The Partners must recognise that by entering into a contract which includes X12 they will be undertaking responsibilities additional to those in the basic NEC contract. They are required to work together as stated in the Partnering Information.

Any dispute (or difference) between Partners who do not have a contract between themselves is resolved by the Core Group. If the Core Group is unable to resolve the issue, then it is resolved under the procedure of the Partner's own contracts. This will be either directly or indirectly with the Client, who will always be involved at some stage in the contractual chain.

There are no direct remedies between the non-contracting Partners for recovering losses suffered by one of them caused by a failure of another. These remedies remain available in each Partner's own contract. Their existence should, however, encourage the parties to resolve any differences that arise.

So how does NEC with Option X12 Partnering compare with other multi-party arrangements? The open structure of X12 is described previously (Figure 12), the closed structure available in other multi-party partnering contracts is shown in Figure 14. Conceptually, there is an argument that supports an approach of the Client engaging key suppliers on the same terms, all financially incentivised and motivated to deliver the project objectives and taking collective responsibility for this. In practice, though, there are some drawbacks when compared with the NEC approach.

- It is very difficult to get multiple suppliers to agree to a single set of words and allocation of risks between them at the same time.
- Whilst there may be provision for parties leaving and new ones arriving after initial agreement, this effectively creates a new contract. There is a question of legality of this in certain jurisdictions, but also the greater practical concern of the time this takes due to the due diligence that is necessitated of settlement of the outgoing party's account and the risk profiles of the accounts of the new and remaining members.
- The risk profile of the likes of designers is very different in this contract as each party is bearing some financial responsibility for the performance of the other parties. For example, an architect may find his financial exposure for his share of potential project cost over-runs of what would ordinarily constitute sub-contractors could be in the order of his whole fee for delivering his services. This is a very different risk profile to the majority of projects an architect, or most suppliers, find themselves in. Mitigating this risk can be very problematic.

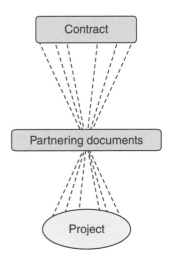

Figure 14. Typical single multi-party contract.

Incentivisation

NEC offers a range of measures from which the parties can select to give best value for any particular project or programme of work. These are present at a bi-party level and there can be common incentives across a number of Partners when the Option X12 Partnering is used. The range of NEC incentives includes matters that affect the likes of time, cost and quality; the following list gives some examples.

- Bonus for early Completion – in ECC there is provision for introducing a bonus for each day the Contractor completes the works ahead of the contractual Completion Date.
- Target cost – in ECC, TSC and PSC the Client can utilise target cost arrangements where, if the supplier delivers the out-turn cost below the level of the final target, the savings are shared according to a pre-agreed formula. A similar sharing arrangement of over-run reciprocates this arrangement.
- KPIs – KPIs can be introduced through Option X12 Partnering and Option X20 for any matter the parties care to agree upon. Examples include the number of Defects, the whole project costs to the Client, the rate of progress of certain works, whether client satisfaction levels were reached, whether the asset is cheaper to operate and maintain than expected, and so on.

Major incentives should be a job done well, reputation and repeat work. It is argued that partnering on one-off projects is difficult as there is no chance of repeat work. The counter argument is that the single most important asset of most organisations is people and that partnering is really just a way of working. If people are encouraged to flourish and achieve the highest standards they can in a constructive and enjoyable environment, then the wasteful sideshow of dispute resolution goes away, job satisfaction increases and the likelihood is that the end product is better than would otherwise have been the case.

The NEC structure provides for a whole range of incentives if the parties believe they will enhance the prospects of improving upon the levels of performance expected.

Key Performance Indicators

NEC provides for KPIs through Option X12 Partnering or Option X20 Key Performance Indicators. The NEC contracts provide for the use of one or the other, but not both at the same time. The NEC approach with KPIs is to promote the concept of continuous improvement. They are therefore not intended to be used as a negative financial adjustment if the targets set are not achieved or bettered. The basic payment structure of each party's NEC contract should provide for where the stipulated performance is not achieved.

It is recommended that the performance of the supplier and his supply chain is monitored and measured against KPIs. This monitoring is especially important on the cost reimbursable Options where achievement and improving upon KPIs will have a direct relationship with, and impact on, cost.

It is necessary to identify and describe the KPIs, including achievement criteria, at the outset and include this information within the tender documents.

Continuous improvement and innovation are the objectives of KPIs with the ultimate aims of reducing costs and improving quality (both in the product at completion and in long-term usage). If the monitoring of the KPIs shows poor performance, the Client and his advisers should use every endeavour to ensure that proper attention and rectification is implemented. However, in the event of continuous failure by the supplier or the supply chain to meet the KPIs, and in the event of quality and performance being severely compromised, the Client may wish to terminate.

Part 1
What is NEC?

Part 2
NEC3 Procurement and Contract Strategies

Part 3
Other Procurement Aspects

There are many KPIs for Consultants and Contractors that have been put in place as industry standards. NEC does not include a list of possible KPIs. NEC provides the means by which the parties can introduce KPIs and promote continuous improvement. This can lead to higher payment to suppliers and a better product for the Client.

Example   Considering the previous comments on multi-party arrangements, incentivisation and KPIs, how can a Client and his suppliers create an environment where, through incentives, his project objectives have the best chance of being realised?

Assume that a Client is building a new hospital and is adopting a prime contracting procurement route. Figure 15 indicates the relationships involved in such a project, although in reality there would be many more suppliers than shown.

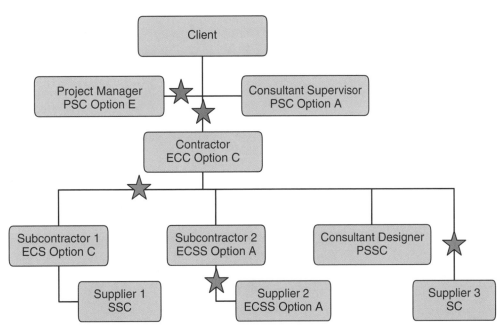

Figure 15. Example of Option X12 Partnering.

The main contract is between the Client and the Contractor, which is an ECC Option C contract. This is a target cost contract. The Client also enters into a contract with a Project Manager to administer the ECC contract on the Client's behalf. A PSC contract is used, with Option E selected due to the uncertainty of definition of duties the Project Manager will provide. The Client also uses the PSC to engage the services of a Supervisor who will check that the materials and workmanship provided by the Contractor accords with the levels specified in the ECC.

The Contractor in turn subcontracts the works. He engages Subcontractor 1 on a similar basis to the terms he holds himself, namely Option C. Subcontractor 1 subsubcontracts part of his works to a supplier for some off-the-shelf items of goods and uses SSC for his contract with Supplier 1. Subcontractor 2 has a fairly straightforward low-risk scope of works and so the Contractor elects to use ECSS Option A, which gives a lump sum for the said works. Again, Subcontractor 2 subsubcontracts the works and this time mirrors his contract by using ECSS Option A. The Contractor also engages the services of a local Designer and for this uses PSC Option C, again a target cost contract. Finally, the Contractor uses the SC to procure some high-value bespoke goods from Supplier 3, which he will install himself.

In the ECC or ECS contracts, a bonus for early Completion can be included. In the Option C contracts under PSC and ECC, there is a financial incentive incorporated by way of the painshare/gainshare formula, based on the final out-turn costs when compared with the final target costs. In Figure 15 the stars again represent the X12 Partners and in this case they comprise the Core Group. This group therefore includes the Client, Project Manager, Contractor, Subcontractor 1, Consultant designer, Supplier 2 and Supplier 3. Supplier 3 is supplying a key M&E component, which is why he is selected to be a Partner. Using X12, the Client and his Partners decide upon a series of collective and individual incentives to optimise supplier performance. These could include the following.

Example incentivisations (using X12)

- If the total cost of the project including all Client costs is less than £3,000,000, 75% of the difference is split between the Partners as follows:
  - 20% to the Contractor
  - 15% to Supplier 3, and so on.
- If the number of notified Defects is less than 100 nr each Partner receives £5,000.
- For Supplier 3, if his M&E equipment achieves the following performance levels for 98% of the time during a three-month period after Completion, he receives £10,000.
- For the Project Manager, if 95% of all compensation events are assessed within the ECC timescales he receives £5,000.

Clearly, an optimum number of incentives should be strived for, enough to make a difference and not too many or of an amount that could potentially compromise the Client's objectives in any way.

Option X20 Key Performance Indicators would be used in bi-party contracts where incentivisation is desired but not by involving multiple parties.

Risk management

NEC anticipates and encourages active risk management. Best practice demands of any well-managed project that it has an up-to-date risk register at the heart of its management procedures. NEC seeks to ensure:

- people use active risk management,
- the risk is allocated to the party best able to manage it and
- the parties have a financial impact of managing the risk successfully.

At the earliest opportunity the project team (whoever it consists of at the time) should prepare a single risk register, which is reflective of all risks surrounding the project. Construction risks will be a part of this, but they will certainly not be the only consideration. As the team develops and grows in knowledge, and perhaps also in size, then one would expect the risk register to develop accordingly. The team should consider the likelihood of a risk's occurrence and the impact should it occur. As best the team can, it should look to avoid, reduce or mitigate certainly the key risks, and have regard to those other risks of far less likelihood or severity. The team should also consider risk ownership. Much is said of shared risks and they are sometimes used to include in a target contract, for example, an allowance for the occurrence of a shared risk. If it does not arise the difference is split according to a pre-determined amount. This can be seen as the equivalent of a contingency for an unknown risk or amount of that risk. NEC does not provide for contingencies in any of its contracts and instead categorises risks in each bi-party contract only as Client or supplier risk. Financial provision should be made for both parties' risks, be it in the price if it is supplier risk or a separate contingency fund if Client risk.

Part 1
What is NEC?

Part 2
NEC3 Procurement and Contract Strategies

Part 3
Other Procurement Aspects

At the point of tendering each package of works, the project team needs to ensure that the risk allocation provided in the chosen NEC contract matches that provided for in the risk register. The contractual risks embedded within each NEC contract can be altered to suit the risk register, if required. If the Client is to contractually own risks beyond those in the standard NEC contract, then additional compensation events or additional Employer's risks can be included in Option Z (additional conditions of contract) in the Contract Data part one. If the supplier is to contractually own risks that are as standard allocated to the Client, this can be achieved by amending the base NEC contractual risk allocation in the additional conditions of contract part of each NEC contract.

As an example of both scenarios, assume a Client has engaged a Contractor to design and build a community centre. The Client has chosen a site which is prone to flooding. After due consideration of the Client's requirements by the project team, which involves the construction of permanent flood barriers, if the adjacent river level during construction rises above a certain level this would flood the site. The likelihood is low but the impact of this event would be high. As this risk sits with the Client in any case for the lifetime of the asset, even after defences are in place, the team members agree that this risk best sits with the Client and this is recorded on the risk register. The ECC is used for this project and this new threshold in contractual risk allocation could be administered by adding an additional compensation event in Option Z (additional conditions of contract) in Contract Data part one to record the level at which the event becomes a compensation event. The river level below this threshold does not give grounds for a compensation event, whereas above this threshold it does.

On the same project, the team highlight physical conditions within the site that are a risk and agree a mitigation plan through extensive ground investigation to minimise both likelihood and impact. The works are D&B and the team considers the risk of physical conditions to be encountered being beyond those expected after such ground investigation should sit with the Contractor. If such risk transfer is desired and agreed then this can be effected by deleting the corresponding compensation event in the ECC, which would be done in Option Z (additional conditions of contract).

Each NEC contract has been drafted with an appropriate and carefully considered risk allocation between the parties to reflect a typical project. This risk allocation should be compared pre-contract to the risk register. If working in an integrated environment where the parties negotiate risks and price, it is reasonable to assume that agreement will be reached when both parties are happy with the risk allocation and the price. In a competitive environment without early Contractor involvement, it rests on the Client and his advisers to decide the risk allocation, and suppliers must have due regard to this when tendering. In the vast majority of contracts it is recommended that the core risk allocation should not be changed, except to the extent allowed by the choice of main and secondary Options and the parameters in the Contract Data.

Post-contract, the risk register should continue to be updated by the project team, some risks will expire and new ones may appear. As the contract is already in existence at this time, new risks will fall into the ownership of the Client or supplier, as determined by the risk allocation in the contract. This does not mean that either party has no further regard for the other party's risks, as demonstrated by the NEC's early warning process.

Where target cost contracts are used under NEC, the target cost itself is deemed to be inclusive not only of the anticipated costs of providing the works together with returns for overheads and profit, but also of the Contractor's risks as provided for in the contract. The occurrence of Contractor's risks does not itself result in a change in the target cost. In terms of payment, however, it is quite a different proposition. The Client pays the Contractor's Defined Cost less Disallowed Costs plus the Fee and therefore the Client will be paying the Defined Cost of certain Contractor's risks. This means the Client is effectively sharing the cost effects of Contractor's risks by means of paying for most of those that occur. This at least has the effect that the target is likely to be a lesser figure than would have been the case under a lump sum contract and both parties care about the occurrence of Contractor's risk as they both have a stake in it.

Part 1
What is NEC?

Part 2
NEC3 Procurement and
Contract Strategies

Part 3
Other Procurement
Aspects

Supply chain management

Supply chain management has many definitions. One definition is the strategic co-ordination of all parties that are involved in delivering the combination of inputs, outputs or outcomes that will meet a specified requirement. It is about bringing to bear the skill and expertise of suppliers to achieve solutions to Client needs. How the suppliers are integrated is important for ensuring that this combined and co-ordinated expertise is offered up to assist in achieving the Client's objectives.

Many Clients actively promote an integrated team approach under a partnering arrangement. Suppliers are expected to bring to the project the benefits of a well-managed supply chain. Supply chains can be fully integrated with common management processes, long term with strategic sets of relationships between a number of organisations or short term with ad hoc structures to deliver one-off projects.

NEC provides an integrated set of contract forms to engage properly the supply chain on common terms with an emphasis on efficient management processes. It is not possible, in the conditions of contract, to address every requirement of every Client on every project or programme in terms of supply chain management. Where this is an essential aspect of a Client's award criteria at tender stage, this should be expressly provided for in the invitation to tender usually by inclusion of appropriate requirements in the 'Information' or 'Scope' sections of the documents.

Operating, maintenance and compliance periods

On some projects Clients will require that for an extended period after Completion the Contractor is to demonstrate that the asset is designed and/or built to meet the required standards. This is also often the case in prime contracting where compliance periods are required and the costs of operating and maintaining the asset are checked.

Different industries and forms of contracts use a variety of wording to cover Defects, operating, maintenance and compliance periods. What NEC means by these definitions and how they are catered for is as follows.

- Defect – broadly defined in each NEC contract as something the supplier has done that does not accord with the stated requirements, which is the Works Information in the ECC, Scope in the PSC, Service Information in the TSC or Goods Information in the SC. In its simplest form, the work done by a Contractor under ECC does not conform with the line, level, tolerance, etc., as stated. The principle the ECC adopts with Defects (similar with other NEC contracts) is the Contractor is given the opportunity to correct the Defect within prescribed timescales. This is unless a proposal to leave the Defect in place with appropriate whole-life consideration is given and accepted. If the Defect is not corrected, then an adjustment is made to the price the Contractor receives. This reflects the cost to the Client of having to engage another Contractor to put the work right.

- Operating period – this is where a supplier operates the Client's asset for a prescribed period of time, sometimes many years. The contract strategy for the operating period could either be through sectional completion under ECC if the operating period is not too long, or use ECC to construct and TSC to operate if this is an extended period. Under ECC, if any works failed the stipulated criteria in terms of construction or operation then this would be classified as a Defect, with the responsibility resting with the Contractor to remedy the problem.

- Maintenance period – this is traditionally the period of, say, one year after a Contractor has completed the works during which he is responsible for correcting latent Defects that arise. Most problems will probably arise in this first year of use. This is covered in the ECC in this way, the period after Completion running

Part 1
What is NEC?

Part 2
NEC3 Procurement and Contract Strategies

Part 3
Other Procurement Aspects

for the prescribed period until the defects date. The 'Maintain' in the DBOM procurement route described earlier passes the responsibility of maintaining the Client's asset in a certain condition for extended timescales. Generally, NEC sees that this would be provided under a TSC, where the asset performance, operating levels, etc., are described in the Service Information and with monies not due to the supplier where performances levels are not reached.

- Compliance period – this is a period of time where, for example, under ECC, the Contractor demonstrates through the likes of take over and performance tests that the asset is performing in accordance with the contracted target levels. If ECC is used for this compliance period then sectional completion could be utilised as before or alternatively this can be part of the period after Completion up to the defects date. On balance, the former is preferred as the works are not said to be complete until the Contractor demonstrates the asset complies with the required performance levels. Whichever route is preferred by Clients, any such non-compliance would be classified a Defect and the procedure associated with this commences. The ECC and SC also provide a secondary Option for low performance damages which provide for where the supplier has provided something not to the upper level of performance required but above the lower level of performance required. The damages reflect the whole-life consequence to a Client of the loss of performance from the required level. The introduction of the damages clause saves the parties from the expense of resolving such a problem through the Courts.

Framework contracts

Many public and private clients set up framework contracts for the supply of works, services or supply. These are often characterised by upwards of three-year relationships that frequently involve extensive selection requirements to determine the desired supplier for that period and means that unsuccessful suppliers have to sit and wait for the next opportunity to come, possibly years later. Because of this, selection of the right supplier is vital and the principles of best practice are adopted to ensure continuous improvement is achieved.

NEC3 provides a Framework Contract (FC) for Clients to use as a head contract in this type of relationship. As drafted, each 'job' is a 'task' that sits within and is carried out under the FC. This is quite different from the TSC and TSSC arrangements, which are term contracts, often used to maintain an asset in a certain state.

For a Client, the FC is used in conjunction with any of the ECC, ECSC, PSC, PSSC, TSC, TSSC, SC or SSC as applicable. The FC does not promise the supplier any work, it effectively says 'as and when I need some work doing, this is how we will manage the process of defining the scope, agreeing the price, what the conditions will be and how the works will be executed'. The FC will also likely include regular supplier meetings, statements that in a multiple supplier framework more work may go to the better suppliers and the inclusion of KPIs to determine who the best suppliers are.

Value management

Value management may be described as a structured approach to the assessment and development of a project to increase the likelihood of achieving those requirements at optimum whole-life value for money. The focus of value management is not on reducing cost but rather on function and value for money. Value engineering is the ongoing process of critically appraising components and processes to determine whether better value alternatives or solutions are available.

NEC expects that the requirements to engage the participants in value management are specified in the Works Information. This is also noted in the guidance of using Option X12 Partnering. It is not the contract that will drive value management but rather the environment that the project participants wish to work within. You cannot force people to come up with outstanding value engineering ideas, this should be embedded in the culture of an organisation. For this reason, NEC does not stipulate the process of doing value management or value engineering as a contract condition.

NEC makes express provision for value management in ECC Options C and D, target cost contracts. If the Contractor proposes a value engineering idea that changes the Works Information to reduce the Contractor's costs, then the target is not changed. In this manner, both Client and Contactor should share in the savings due to the target cost share mechanism.

Novation

A Client may need to employ a Designer, for example to provide drawings for the purposes of obtaining planning permission, before a construction Contractor can be appointed. If the contract strategy is for a D&B arrangement, with the Contractor to have full responsibility for the design, it will be necessary to transfer the benefit of the Designer's contract from the Client to the Contractor. The legal process for doing this is known as novation, and is usually achieved by the parties executing a short deed in which they agree to the transfer. The process is not without problems, for example arguments over design errors, unknown to one or both parties, which exist at the time of transfer.

NEC does not expressly provide for novation as this process does not follow the principles of good management practice. Generally, novation will take place under a PSC contract. The Scope, risks and constraints need properly drafting and understanding in order for any Designer to understand their responsibilities and to arrive at an acceptable price for undertaking the service. NEC considers that the end product of novation is effectively no different to the Designer entering into a contract with the new Client from the outset. For this reason, there is no shortcut handover NEC document as each contract placed under NEC should be thoroughly understood by both parties, regardless of how or why the two parties finished up together in contract.

Early Contractor Involvement

Early Contractor Involvement (ECI) is an increasingly popular method of engaging a Contractor and maybe some of his supply chain, at any earlier stage in a project than is traditionally the case. Historically, the Designer designs and the builder builds, and the two rarely came together to challenge one another's assumptions to ensure the best solution for the project was arrived at. D&B goes some way towards improving the integration of design and construction, but the success of the end product often rested on how good the brief was in the first place. ECI started life as an unpaid way of bringing Contractors' expertise to the table, and in turn Contractors hoped this would help secure them the construction works. This was an unsatisfactory approach and de-valued the contribution that a Contractor provides. Most Clients are now happy to pay for that early advice, as they would for a Consultant, and one expects this creates the right circumstances to bring high quality input at the earliest stage in the project's life cycle to bring maximum value.

ECI can be used in a two- or three-stage model. It can be used on a minimalist basis by bidding a job then bringing the successful Contractor on board to see if any value engineering ideas can be brought to the project, albeit late in the day. On the other extreme, it can be used to help create a sound business case for a project, to jointly

Part 1
What is NEC?

Part 2
NEC3 Procurement and Contract Strategies

Part 3
Other Procurement Aspects

appraise risk, value, buildability issues, design and whole-life solutions, to negotiate a price for the works and then to execute the construction works. The early work can be initiated over one, two or more stages, with construction being the final stage (unless of course the project also involves operation and/or maintenance). If at the end of any of the early stages the project's business case is not sound or the price is too high, the Client is able to stop the project without facing a claim for losses by the Contractor who was anticipating taking the project through construction.

Clients use different NEC contracts in different ways to achieve the same goal. There are several right ways, but at all times Clients and suppliers need to have regard to the legal procurement rules that govern contracts. The following are examples of the different approaches.

- Use ECC Option E cost reimbursement up to the point when there is sufficient project definition to agree a lump sum or target cost for the works.
- Place a series of contracts all under ECC. Use Option E cost reimbursement for the early stages of work and, when a negotiated price is acceptable, place the construction contract under (usually) a target cost or lump sum basis.
- Place two or more contracts in sequence. Use PSC Option E cost reimbursement for the early stages of work and, when a negotiated price is acceptable, place the construction contract under ECC, usually a target cost or lump sum basis.

Opportunity/cost curves demonstrate the later a supplier is brought in using this process, the lower will be the benefits that may be attained. How ECI and NEC are implemented is usually down to Client preference and legal rules governing procurement. The NEC is flexible enough to be used in a number of combinations to achieve the desired outcome.

Sustainability

The NEC Panel has taken the view that a complex issue such as the imposition of sustainability, or perhaps other socially desirable outcomes, is a matter for detailed definition in the ECC Works Information (or the equivalent in other NEC3 contracts). These outcomes are mostly the subject of developing and complex technical requirements, the definition of which will be project specific. Given they are predominantly technical they are best included in the technical specification, such as the ECC Works Information, and drafted to suit the nature of the project. The proven management processes of the chosen NEC contract would then help to ensure the planned outcomes were achieved.

Part 1
What is NEC?

Part 2
NEC3 Procurement and
Contract Strategies

Part 3
Other Procurement
Aspects